Cambridge Lower Secondary
Science

ENGLISH LANGUAGE SKILLS WORKBOOK 8

Mary Jones & Sally Burbeary

CAMBRIDGE
UNIVERSITY PRESS

University Printing House, Cambridge CB2 8BS, United Kingdom

One Liberty Plaza, 20th Floor, New York, NY 10006, USA

477 Williamstown Road, Port Melbourne, VIC 3207, Australia

314–321, 3rd Floor, Plot 3, Splendor Forum, Jasola District Centre, New Delhi – 110025, India

103 Penang Road, #05–06/07, Visioncrest Commercial, Singapore 238467

Cambridge University Press is part of the University of Cambridge.

It furthers the University's mission by disseminating knowledge in the pursuit of education, learning and research at the highest international levels of excellence.

www.cambridge.org
Information on this title: www.cambridge.org/9781108799058

© Cambridge University Press 2021

First published 2014
Second edition 2021

20 19 18 17 16 15 14 13 12 11 10 9 8 7 6 5

Printed in Malaysia by Vivar Printing

A catalogue record for this publication is available from the British Library

ISBN 978-1-108-79905-8 Paperback with Digital Access (1 year)

Additional resources for this publication at www.cambridge.org/delange

> Contents

English skills and support

1 Respiration

2 Properties of materials

3 Forces and energy

Contents

8 Chemical reactions

9 Magnetism

> How to use this book

This workbook will help you to understand and use the English that is involved while learning science.

It will help you to:

- understand what you read in your science books, and what your teacher tells you during the lessons

- talk to other learners during your science lessons in English, using the correct vocabulary

- understand questions that you are asked by your teacher or in a test

- speak or write answers to science questions that say clearly what you mean.

This workbook contains an **English skills and support** section. This contains information about English grammar and vocabulary to help you with science. You can use the reference section at any time you need help with English while studying science.

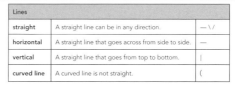

This workbook provides questions for you to practise what you have learnt in class. There is a topic to match each topic in your Learner's Book and exercises in each topic. You can use the English skills and support section to help you as you complete the exercises.

Exercise 2 Writing two or more sentences in an answer

Sometimes, a question needs a slightly longer answer than usual. In this exercise, you practise writing your own sentences to answer some 'Explain' questions.

Look at **Command words** in the *English skills and support* section for information about command words.

Write at least **two** sentences to answer each of these three questions. Make sure that your second sentence has some new information in it and is not just the first sentence written in a different way.

a Explain why it is easier to cut an apple with a sharp knife than a blunt knife.

....

....

....

....

b Explain what you need to know in order to calculate the pressure that an object is producing on the floor.

> English skills and support

This book is to help you with English skills when you are studying science. The *English skills and support* section gives you information about important topics in English that you will use in science. You can use this section at any time you need help with English while studying science.

In this English reference section, there is information about English grammar and vocabulary to help you with science.

Many different grammatical words will be explained in the English language reference section.

Connecting words

Connecting words help you to join two pieces of information together in different ways.

In science, we often need to talk about more than one thing. We can join two ideas together with connecting words, for example: *and, but, because, so*. These are called connectives. Connectives are like glue – they stick two ideas together.

There are many connecting words in English and they do different things in sentences.

Connective		What it is used for
and	⟶	connecting two positives together
or	⟶	connecting two negatives together
but	⟶	connecting a positive and a negative together
because	⟶	giving a reason why
so	⟶	giving the result of a situation

Here are some examples.

and		*positive*	+	*positive*
	Roots are usually underground		and	anchor the plant in the ground.
but		*positive*	+	*negative*
	The roots underground continue to live		but	the parts of the plant above ground might die in harsh conditions.
because		*fact or situation*	+	*why*
	Plants can absorb minerals from soil		because	they have roots.
so		*fact or situation*	+	*result*
	Plants have roots		so	they can absorb minerals from the soil.

Command words

Science questions often start with 'Name', 'State', 'Describe' or 'Explain'. You need to know how to answer these questions correctly.

Command words	Answer
Name	Give the **name** of the person, object or animal.
State	Give brief information.
Describe	Say **what** happens.
Explain	Say **why** something happens.

For example:

Question: **Name** a compound.

Answer: Water.

Question: **State** the features of a compound.

Answer: A compound has more than one type of atom, which are joined tightly together.

Question: **Describe** what happens when iron is heated with sulfur.

Answer: The iron and sulfur react together to form a new substance. The iron atoms bond with the sulfur atoms to make iron sulfide.

Question: **Explain** why metals oxidise.

Answer: Many metals oxidise because of a chemical reaction of the metal surface with the oxygen present in the air.

Comparative and superlative adjectives

This section helps you to do *two* things.

It helps you to talk about:

- the differences between things (comparative adjectives)

- an object expressing the extreme quality of that thing in a group of objects (superlative adjectives).

Scientists often want to compare two or more things.

For example: feathers and leaves are *lighter* than stones and rocks.

Comparative adjectives

Comparative adjectives are formed by adding *-er* to shorter adjectives and *more* before longer adjectives. The number of **syllables** in a word helps you to choose whether to use *-er* or *more*. A syllable is the number of sounds in a word. For example, 'gas' has one syllable, 'copper' has two syllables and 'magnetic' has three syllables. Be careful with the spelling rules when forming comparative adjectives. Notice that 'than' is used after the comparative adjective.

	Form	Example sentence	Spelling notes
One syllable adjectives	tall + er fast + er	An adult is *taller* than a young child. A leopard runs *faster* than an antelope.	For most adjectives, just add *-er* to the end.
	close + r large + r	The particles in a solid are *closer* together than in a gas. A molecule is *larger* than an atom.	Adjectives that end in *-e*, just add *-r* to the end.
	big + er hot + er	Jupiter is *bi**gg**er* than Mars. Venus is *ho**tt**er* than Neptune.	If the last three letters of the adjective end in consonant, vowel, consonant, double the last letter before adding *-er*. Remember vowels are A, E, I, O, U and consonants are all of the remaining letters of the alphabet. There are exceptions to the rule, for example, words ending in 'w', such as: low and slow become *lower* and *slower*.
Two syllable adjectives ending in -y	heavy + er healthy + er	A brick is heav*ier* than a feather. Fruit is health*ier* than chocolate.	For adjectives ending in 'y', change the 'y' to 'i'.
Two syllable adjectives **not** ending in -y	more + common more + active	At night bats are *more common* than most birds. Bats are *more active* at night than most birds.	
Long adjectives of three or more syllables	more + reactive more + addictive	Magnesium is *more reactive* than nickel. Nicotine is *more addictive* than caffeine.	

You can also compare things that are the same: for example, 'Lemon juice is as acidic as vinegar.'

You can also show how one thing affects another.

Here are some examples.

- The greater the amplitude of the sound wave, the louder the sound.

- The more you exercise, the harder your muscles work.

Be careful when using 'bigger' or 'larger' and 'greater.' Generally, 'bigger' and 'larger' mean the same and are used to talk about the physical size of objects, animals and people. 'Greater' has a similar meaning, but it is also used to talk about the value of something, for example 'the force is greater'.

Superlative adjectives

In science, you may also want to say what is at the top or the bottom of a range of things. Superlative adjectives say what is at the top and the bottom of a range. Notice that you always put 'the' before superlative adjectives

Remember, you make a superlative adjective by:

- adding -est to the end of short adjectives (hard, cold, large, small)

  For example: Diamonds are *the hardest* natural substance on Earth.

- or adding *the most* before longer adjectives (reactive, conductive, reflective)

  For example: *The most conductive* element is silver.

Be careful! Words of two syllables (sounds) can use both -est and *the most*.

For two-syllable adjectives ending in 'y' change 'y' to 'i' and add -est (heavy – *the heaviest*).

For adjectives of two or more syllables **not** ending in 'y', add *the most* before the adjective (active – *the most* active; reactive – *the most* reactive).

Be aware that some adjectives are irregular. This means they don't follow the usual rules.

Irregular adjectives		
Adjective	Comparative	Superlative
far	further	the furthest
few	fewer	the fewest
little	less	the least
many	more	the most

The language of science experiments

When doing scientific experiments, you often use the words *observations*, *results*, *conclusions* and *explanation*. You need to be clear about the differences between them.

observation	Something that you notice, using your senses.
result	What you find out in your experiment: results are often numerical data.
conclusion	Your decision about what your results mean: a conclusion is often an answer to the question your experiment investigated, or a decision about whether your hypothesis is supported or disproved.
explanation	Why or how you reached this conclusion: you use your scientific understanding to give reasons.

Making predictions

A prediction is a guess about what you expect to happen in the future, based on your observations.

You can use **will** and **might** to make predictions.

Will and **might** are followed by the infinitive of the verb without "to", for example:

It **will** snow this winter.
It **might** snow this winter.

Will shows that we are very sure:
A plant that has light and water **will** grow well.

I think the universal indicator **will** turn red when I dip it in lemon juice.

Might shows we are less sure:

Eating too much red meat **might** cause heart disease.

It is raining and the sun is coming out. We **might** see a rainbow.

Will and **might** are the same for all people and objects, for example:

I, you, he, she, it, they, we **will** predict the result accurately.

I, you, he, she, it, they, we **might** not get an accurate result.

It is common to use **I think**…, **I don't think**… and **Do you think**…? to introduce predictions when we speak.

For example:

I think water will turn to ice at zero degrees Celsius.

I think silver might melt at a lower temperature than iron.

I don't think aluminium will oxidise in water.

Do you think this experiment will work well?

Do you think this experiment might fail?

Note: we cannot use might with I don't think.

Modal verbs

> Modal verbs are a special type of verb that go before normal verbs in a sentence. Modal verbs show that things are *certain*, *probable*, *possible* or *impossible*.

There are many modal verbs and each one has a different function or functions.

Here are some of the most common modal verbs.

can	This modal verb shows: • an **ability** to do something • that something is **possible**.
 Sound **can** travel through air. (Sound has the **ability** to travel through air.) Water **can** be a solid, liquid or a gas. (It is **possible** for water to be a solid, liquid or a gas.)	
cannot (can't)	This means the opposite. It means: • you are **not able** to do something • that something is **not possible**.

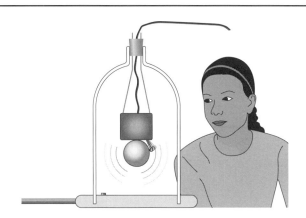

Sound **can't** travel through a vacuum. (Sound does **not** have the **ability** to travel through a vacuum.)

When a solution is saturated, the solvent **can't** dissolve any more solute. (It is **not possible** to dissolve any more solute.)

might	This means there is **a chance** it could happen.

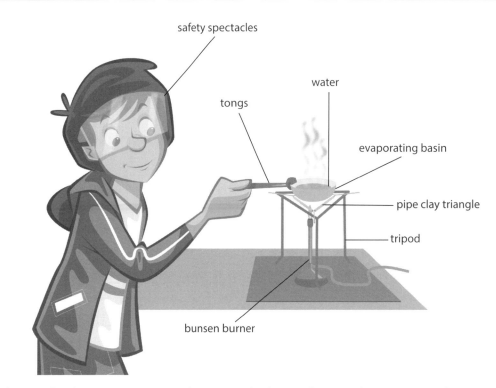

When I do this experiment, there **might** be a chemical reaction. (There is **a chance** that there will be a chemical reaction.)

might not	This means the opposite. It means that **perhaps** it won't happen.
You **might not** get the result you predicted. (**Perhaps** the result will be different from what you expected.)	

must	This is a strong modal verb and it means that something is **essential** to do (you **can't** say no).
You **must** wear goggles when mixing chemicals. (It is **essential** to avoid accidents.)	
must not (mustn't)	This means the opposite. It means that it is **essential** not to do something.
You **must not** spill chemicals on your skin. (It is essential **not** to do this as it is very dangerous.)	

should	Use this modal verb to: <ul><li>give **advice**</li><li>show something you **expect** will happen.</li></ul>
You **should** eat a balanced diet to be healthy. (I **advise** you to do this.) Water **should** freeze when the temperature is below 0 °C. (You **expect** water to freeze when the temperature is below 0 °C.)	
should not (shouldn't)	This means the opposite. It means: <ul><li>**advise not** to do something</li><li>something that you **don't expect** to happen.</li></ul>
You **shouldn't** eat too much fatty food. (I **advise** you **not** to do this.) Gold **shouldn't** oxidise in air. (You **don't expect** gold to oxidise in air.)	

Prepositions

Prepositions are usually short words, for example: *in, on, at, by, from, to, out.* Each preposition has a particular meaning and it is important you know how they are used in sentences. There are other prepositions in English that can be used in different ways to the examples included here, and the exercises in this workbook will help you learn about some of those other uses.

In, at, on are common prepositions. You can use these prepositions to talk about time or place.

Prepositions – time	Usage	Examples
in	duration of time	I will check the temperature **in** five minutes (in the future). I will check the plant growth **in** three days (in the future). I wake up early **in** the morning. I often go on holiday **in** the summer.
at	a precise time	The sun sets **at** 6 o'clock. I am learning science **at** the moment. Nocturnal animals hunt **at** night.
on	days and dates	I have football practice **on** Wednesday. My birthday is **on** 10th September.

Prepositions – place	Usage	Examples
in	in a space or area, or inside something	I live **in** a town/country. I plant seeds **in** a garden. Fish live **in** the water. My lessons are **in** a school. (Inside the building.)
at	a point or particular place	I write my notes **at** my desk. I write my name **at** the top. I meet my friends **at** school. (**At** this place.)
on	a surface	My book is **on** the table. Wood floats **on** water. My chair is **on** the floor.

Prepositions	Usage	Examples
through	through and along are similar; through means moving from one side to the other in a three dimensional object	I run **through** the tunnel. Water flows **through** the pipe. Oxygen passes **through** the lungs. I can see **through** the hole.
along	move in line with something (the distance or length travelled is the main idea)	The ball travels **along** the ground. Marcus measured Zara's heart rate as she walked quickly **along** the road.
down	moving to a lower level	A rock sinks **down** to the bottom of a river. Gravity: what goes up, must come **down**.
up	moving to a higher level	Wood floats **up** to the surface of a river. Mercury rises in a thermometer as the temperature goes **up**.
between	in or into an area that separates two people, places or objects	Put a light bulb **between** a battery and a switch to make a simple circuit. The Earth is **between** Venus and Mars.
from	comes *from* a source	Scientists extract metal ore **from** rocks. Arteries carry blood away **from** the heart.
for	intended *for* something or a purpose	Roughage is another name **for** fibre. An ammeter is used **for** measuring electrical current.
of	relationship between things	Gold is a type **of** metal. The heart is part **of** the circulatory system.
by	how something is done the cause of something	You can make tea **by** diffusing tea leaf particles in hot water. (This is how you make tea.) In smokers, cancer is caused **by** tar in cigarettes. (Tar is the cause of cancer.)

Phrasal verbs

Phrasal verbs are made up of a verb followed by a preposition.
Prepositions are usually short words, for example: *in, on, at, by, from, up*. Phrasal verbs are used a lot in English and science. Each phrasal verb can have many meanings, but these are common uses of phrasal verbs with 'out' in science.

Verbs used without a preposition have one meaning, but when you add a preposition to the verb it has a different meaning. *Carry* and *carry out* are used a lot in science, so it is important to know the difference.

Verb	Preposition	Meaning	Example
carry	out	to do an activity	I **carried out** the experiment on my own.
give	out	emit	Some chemical reactions **give out** heat.
spread	out	to open, arrange or place something over a large area	When potassium manganate (VII) is placed in water, the particles **spread out** and mix with the water particles.
find	out	discover	I want to **find out** if paper aluminium is magnetic.
run	out	use every last available part or piece/having nothing left	The engine will stop if it **runs out** of fuel.
mix	up	confuse	Don't **mix up** the meaning of reflection and refraction.
make	up	create	The colour magenta is **made up** of red and blue.

'To' is a very common preposition and is used in many different ways. Here are some verbs that are followed by 'to'.

Verb	Preposition	Example
join, attach, add	to (something or someone)	**Add** hydrogen **to** oxygen and it makes water. The muscles in your forearm cross the elbow and **attach to** the humerus. In a battery, **join** the cathode **to** the positive terminal, and the anode **to** the negative terminal.
introduce	to (something or someone)	The grey squirrel was **introduced to** the UK in the 1890s. Arun, I would like to **introduce** you **to** Zara.

Graphs

You need to know the names of the different parts of a graph.

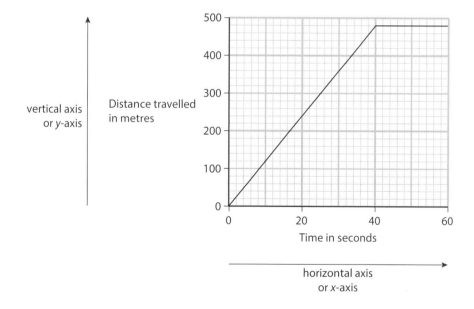

Lines		
straight	A straight line can be in any direction.	— \ /
horizontal	A straight line that goes across from side to side.	—
vertical	A straight line that goes from top to bottom.	|
curved line	A curved line is not straight.	(

Singular and plural

Singular means one thing.

Plural means two or more things.

A **verb** describes an action, state or event.

The verb 'to be'

Use the verb *is* with single and uncountable nouns. For example: A heart *is* an organ.

Use the verb *are* with plural nouns. For example: There *are many* organs in the human body.

Other verbs

Who or what	Verbs
I, you, we, they	look, explain, change, transfer, use
it, she, he	looks, explains, changes, transfers, uses

If you start a sentence with *It*, *She* or *He*, you must put an 's' on the end of the verb.

It is easy to get confused with the letter 's' at the end of English words.

Remember: an 's' on the end of a noun usually makes it plural (for example: 1 vein, 2 vein**s**).

Remember: an 's' on the end of a verb makes it agree with *it*, *she*, *he* (for example: it reflect**s**, she experiment**s**).

Uncountable nouns describe things that are impossible to count, for example water, sand and oxygen. Uncountable nouns behave like *it*, *she*, *he* or singular things, and we add an 's' to the end of verbs that follow these words.

Be careful, there are some irregular plural nouns, for example: 1 cactus, 2 cacti and 1 species, 2 species.

Active and passive

You will see sentences using **active verbs** and **passive verbs** in science. Sometimes you need to use passive verbs, but active sentences are easier to understand.

Active verbs

Use active verbs in sentences to give direct and clear information.

Structure: Who does/did what.

Examples:

- I observe the chemical reaction.
- He dissolves sugar in water.
- She can use indicator paper to test acidity.
- The reaction produced hydrogen gas.

Passive verbs

Passive verbs in sentences are sometimes more confusing for learners of English.

Structure: Something is/are/was/were done by whom or what. It is possible not to include who did the action if it is not important who did it.

Example:

- The chemical reaction is observed (by me).
- The sugar is dissolved in water (by him).
- Indicator paper can be used (by her) to test acidity.
- Hydrogen gas was produced by the reaction.

Changing active to passive

it, she, he

Active		
Who/what	**verb**	**What**
We	*measure*	the distance.
She	*measures*	the distances.
Passive		
What	**is/are + past participle**	**Who/what**
The distance	*is measured*	by us.
The distances	*are measured*	by them.

Notice how the word order changes when you change active to passive.

1 Respiration

> 1.1 The human respiratory system

Exercise 1 Parts of the respiratory system

> This exercise gives you practice in naming and spelling the parts of the respiratory system.

The diagram shows the head and chest cavity of a person.

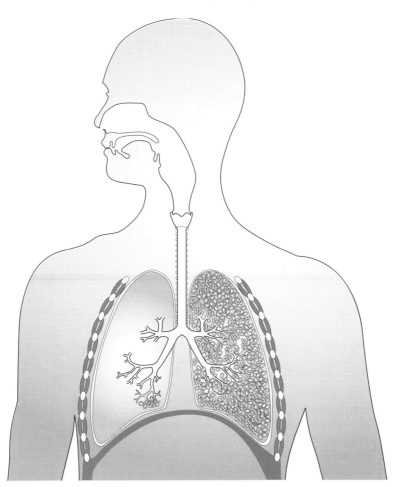

Choose the word or phrase that matches each description. Choose from the list.
Copy the words carefully – do not make any spelling mistakes!

air sac   bronchus   bronchioles   cartilage

larynx   respiratory system   trachea   vocal cords

a   all the organs that work together to help oxygen to get into the body:

....

b   the tube that takes air from the back of the mouth down into the chest; it is

sometimes called the windpipe ....

c   one of two tubes that branches from the trachea

....

d   an organ at the top of the trachea, which contains the vocal cords; it is

sometimes called the voicebox ....

e   a tiny, air-filled space inside the lungs ....

f   the trachea is surrounded by rings of this, to support it

....

g   bands of muscle that stretch across the larynx; they vibrate to make sounds

....

h   tubes that carry air from a bronchus to the air sacs in the lungs

....

Exercise 2 True or false?

This exercise gives you practice in writing positive and negative sentences, as well as checking your understanding of the respiratory system.

If the statement is true, tick (✓) it.

If the statement is false, draw a cross (✗). Then correct the statement by writing a positive or negative sentence.

For example:

The heart is part of the respiratory system.   ☒

The heart is not part of the respiratory system.

a   Respiration is a chemical reaction that happens in every living cell.   ☐

    ....

b   Aerobic respiration does not use oxygen.   ☐

    ....

c   The vocal cords are inside the bronchus.   ☐

    ....

d   The plural of bronchus is bronchioles.   ☐

    ....

e   The lungs do not contain air sacs.   ☐

    ....

> 1.2 Gas exchange

Exercise 1 Using connecting words

In this exercise, you choose the best connecting word to complete sentences about gas exchange.

Look at **Connecting words** in the *English skills and support* section for information about connecting words.

Choose a connecting word to complete each sentence. Choose from the following words. Use each word at least once.

and   **because**   **but**   **so**

a   Oxygen can easily diffuse from the alveoli into the capillaries .... they are very close together.

b   Carbon dioxide is produced in all the cells in the body by respiration, ... expired air contains more carbon dioxide than inspired air.

c   A large volume of air passes through the trachea, ... gas exchange does not happen there.

d   Gas exchange is the movement of oxygen into the blood .... the movement of carbon dioxide out of the blood.

e   An analogy is a comparison between one thing and another, ... the two things are not exactly the same.

Exercise 2 Answering questions

It is important to do what the command word in a question asks you to do. In this exercise, you practise responding to three different command words.

a   Name the substance inside red blood cells that helps them to carry oxygen.

....

b   Describe how oxygen moves from the alveoli into the blood.

....

....

c   Explain why we can use limewater to compare how much carbon dioxide there is in inspired air and expired air.

....

....

....

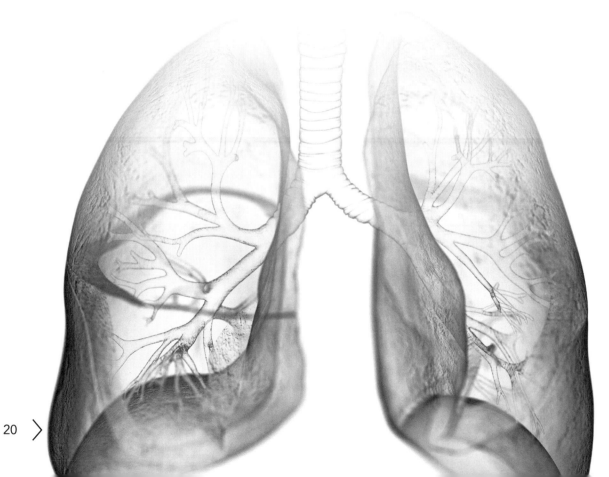

> 1.3 Breathing

Exercise 1 Comparatives.

This exercise gives you practice in describing what happens when we breathe in and breathe out. You have to think of a comparative word to complete each description.

Look at **Comparative and superlative adjectives** in the *English skills and support* section for information about comparatives.

Complete the sentences, using suitable comparative words.

a   Arun can push more water out of the bottle than Marcus, showing that the

capacity of his lungs is .... than Marcus's.

b   In general, the .... a person's lungs, the less air they can breathe

out in one breath.

c   When we breathe out, the diaphragm relaxes and makes the space inside the

chest cavity ....

d   When we are breathing out, the pressure in the chest cavity is ....

than the pressure of the air outside the body.

e   When we breathe in, the diaphragm contracts and makes the pressure inside

the chest cavity ....

Exercise 2 Opposites

This exercise will help you to understand how we breathe in and out, and to use suitable words in your descriptions.

Complete the sentences by writing a word or phrase that is the opposite of the one in **bold**.

a Fill the bottle with water while it is the **right way up**, and then turn it

....

b The intercostal muscles **contract** when we breathe in, and .... when we breathe out.

c When the volume in the chest cavity **increases**, the pressure

....

d The ribs move **upwards** when we breathe in, and .... when we breathe out.

e In the syringe, the balloon **deflates** when I push the plunger in and

.... when I pull the plunger out.

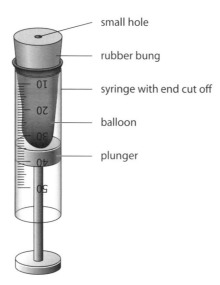

small hole

rubber bung

syringe with end cut off

balloon

plunger

〉 1.4 Respiration

Exercise 1 Observations, results, conclusions and explanations

> This exercise will help you to sort out the differences between an observation, a result, a conclusion and an explanation.

Look at **The language of science experiments** in the *English skills and support* section for information about observations, results, conclusions and explanations.

Sofia set up this apparatus.

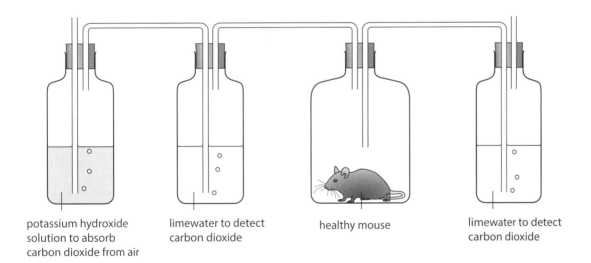

potassium hydroxide solution to absorb carbon dioxide from air

limewater to detect carbon dioxide

healthy mouse

limewater to detect carbon dioxide

Sofia noticed that the limewater in the left-hand container did not go cloudy, even after a long time. After about 5 minutes, the limewater in the right-hand container went cloudy. The mouse appeared to be perfectly comfortable. Sofia thought that her experiment showed that the mouse produced carbon dioxide.

a What **observations** did Sofia make?

....

....

....

....

b Describe the **results** of Sofia's experiment.

....

....

....

c What was Sofia's **conclusion**?

....

....

....

d Write an **explanation** of how this apparatus works.

....

....

....

....

Exercise 2 Modal verbs

Modal verbs tell us about certainties and possibilities. In this exercise, you think about respiration and practise using modal verbs.

Look at **Modal verbs** in the *English skills and support* section for information about modal verbs.

Choose the best word or words to complete each sentence.
Choose from these words:

    might   **might not**   **must**   **must not**

a   Cells .... have mitochondria so that they can carry out aerobic respiration.

b   Cells .... be provided with glucose so that they can carry out aerobic respiration.

c   If you do the experiment using the apparatus with the mouse in it, you

    .... take the mouse out if it looks uncomfortable.

d   If seeds are not given enough oxygen, they .... germinate.

e   If I do the experiment again, my results .... be exactly the same.

> 1.5 Blood

Exercise 1 Writing sentences about an analogy

> We use analogies to help us to understand a structure or a process.
> An analogy compares the structure or process to something familiar.
> In this exercise, you practise writing complete sentences.

The way that water flows through a pipe can be used as an analogy to help us to think about how blood flows through blood vessels.

a   Describe how blood vessels are similar to a plastic water pipe.

    ....

    ....

b   Describe how blood vessels are different from a plastic pipe.

    ....

    ....

c   Describe how blood is similar to water.

    ....

    ....

d   Describe how blood is different from water.

    ....

    ....

Exercise 2 Vocabulary

There are many new words in this topic. This exercise helps you to check that you remember what each of them means.

Draw a line from each word to its meaning.

Words	Meanings
blood plasma	a red substance inside red blood cells
red blood cells	microorganisms that cause disease
white blood cells	the liquid part of blood
haemoglobin	cells that help to destroy pathogens
oxyhaemoglobin	a bright red compound formed when oxygen combines with haemoglobin
pathogens	chemicals, produced by white blood cells, that kill pathogens
phagocytosis	taking something into a cell and digesting it
antibodies	cells whose function is to transport oxygen

2 ▶ Properties of materials

> 2.1 Dissolving

Exercise 1 Using prepositions

> Often, it is the small words that can cause problems. In this exercise, you choose the correct preposition to make each sentence make sense.

Look at **Prepositions** and **Phrasal verbs** in the *English skills and support* section for information about prepositions.

Choose the correct prepositions to complete these sentences.
Choose from these prepositions.

in	out	through	to	up	with

a Sugar can dissolve .... water.

b It is important not to mix .... the meaning of the words solvent and solute.

c You can make a copper sulfate solution by adding copper sulfate

.... water.

d If a substance is transparent, we can see .... it.

e If we get an opaque mixture when we add this substance to water, we know

that it is not soluble .... water.

f The results of the experiment were unusual because they were ....
of the expected range.

Exercise 2 Observations, results, conclusions and explanations

This exercise gives you practice in identifying observations, results and conclusions, and giving explanations.

Look at **The language of science experiments** in the *English skills and support* section for information about observations, results, conclusions and explanations.

Zara does an experiment to find out if mass is conserved when one substance dissolves in another substance.

- Zara measures the mass of a beaker of water. The reading on the scale is 49.5 g.

- Zara adds 3 g of substance A to the water in the beaker and stirs it until it completely dissolves, forming a transparent solution. She measures the mass again, and finds that it is 52.5 g.

a   What **observations** does Zara make?

   ....

   ....

   ....

b What **results** does Zara collect?

....

....

....

c What **conclusion** can Zara make from her observations and results?

....

....

....

d Write some sentences, or make a labelled drawing, to **explain** what happened in Zara's experiment.

....

....

....

....

....

› 2.2 Solutions and solubility

Exercise 1 The more ..., the more

> This exercise will make you think hard about solubility, and also practise using a sentence structure that we often use in science.

Complete each sentence.

a   The more concentrated a solution, the .... solute is dissolved in the solvent.

b   The more insoluble a substance is, the .... of it will dissolve.

c   The less soluble a substance is, the .... solute is present in a saturated solution.

d   The less solute is dissolved in a solution, the .... dilute the solution is.

e   The more I stir the mixture of the solvent and solute, the .... time the solute will take to dissolve.

f   The greater the solubility of a substance, the .... of it will dissolve in a particular volume of solvent.

Exercise 2 Writing two or more sentences in an answer

Sometimes, a question needs a slightly longer answer than usual. In this exercise, you practise writing your own sentences to answer some 'Explain' questions.

Look at **Command words** in the *English skills and support* section for information about command words.

Write at least **two** sentences to answer each of these three questions. Make sure that your second sentence has some new information in it and is not just the first sentence written in a different way.

a Explain the meaning of the term 'saturated solution'.

....

....

....

....

b Explain why most solutes are more soluble in hot water than in cold water.

....

....

....

....

c Explain the difference between a concentrated solution and a dilute solution.

....

....

....

....

> 2.3 Planning a solubility investigation

Exercise 1 Vocabulary for planning experiments

When you plan an experiment, you need to think about variables. In this exercise, you check that you know the correct words for the different kinds of variable in an investigation.

Arun and Marcus want to compare the solubility of two salts. They decide to find out if sodium chloride is more soluble in water than calcium chloride.

a   What is the **independent variable** in their investigation?
Tick (✓) the correct answer.

the mass of the salt that will dissolve in the water ☐

the salts that they use ☐

the temperature ☐

the volume of water that they use ☐

b   What is the **dependent variable** in their investigation?
Tick (✓) the correct answer.

the mass of the salt that will dissolve in the water ☐

the salts that they use ☐

the temperature ☐

the volume of water that they use ☐

c   What are the important control variables in the investigation?
Tick (✓) **two** boxes.

the mass of the salt that will dissolve in the water ☐

the salts that they use ☐

the temperature ☐

the volume of water that they use ☐

d Name the apparatus that the boys will use to measure the mass of the salts.

....

e Name the apparatus that the boys will use to measure the volume of water.

....

Exercise 2 Range, interval and units

In this exercise, you practise reading and understanding information about an experiment. You also need to use your own knowledge about apparatus and units.

Sofia and Zara do an experiment to find out how temperature affects the mass of a salt that can dissolve in water.

- They measure $100 \, cm^3$ of water into a beaker.
- They put the beaker into a water bath at 25 °C.
- They add the salt to the water and measure the mass that can dissolve.

They repeat these three steps using temperatures of 35 °C, 45 °C, 55 °C, 65 °C and 75 °C

a What is the **range** of the temperatures that Sofia and Zara use in their experiment?

....

b What is the **interval** between the temperatures at which they take their readings?

....

c State the apparatus and the unit that the girls use to measure the volume of water.

apparatus...

unit...

d State the apparatus and the unit that they use to measure the temperature of the water.

apparatus...

unit..

e State the apparatus and the unit that they use to measure the mass of salt.

apparatus...

unit..

〉 2.4 Paper chromatography

Exercise 1 Putting words in the correct sequence

In this exercise, you use your understanding of chromatography to sort out some mixed up sentences.

Look at **Comparative and superlative adjectives** in the *English skills and support* section for information about comparatives and superlatives.

In each of these sentences, one or two words are in the wrong sequence (order).

Rewrite the sentence, with the words in the correct sequence.

For example:

We can find out how colours many different there are in ink, using chromatography.

We can find out how many different colours there are in ink, using chromatography.

a The chromatogram shows that this permanent marker three colours has in it.

....

....

b The solvent front is the solvent level that the highest reaches on the chromatogram.

....

....

c I know that this dye is a pure substance not because there are three different spots on the chromatogram.

....

....

d The substance that is furthest soluble travels most on the chromatography paper.

....

....

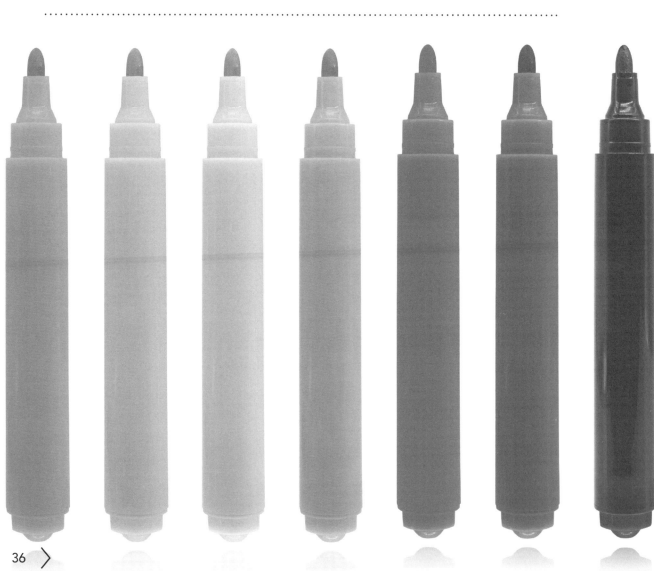

Exercise 2 Comparatives and superlatives

Marcus made a chromatogram using ink from five different coloured pens.

The diagram shows the results.

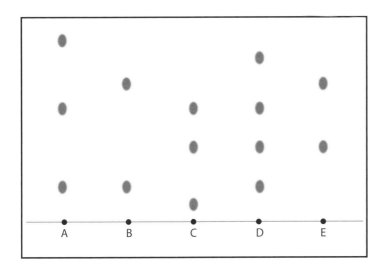

Complete the sentences, using some of these words.

     fewer   **further**   **more**   **the least**   **the most**

a   There were .... different colours in pen **D** than in pen **A**.

b   Pen **D** had .... different colours.

c   Pens **B** and **E** had .... different colours than the other pens.

d   One of the colours in Pen **A** travelled .... than any of the other colours.

e   One of the colours in Pen **C** travelled .... distance of all the colours.

3 ▶ Forces and energy

> 3.1 Forces and motion

Exercise 1 Opposites

In this exercise you check your understanding of balanced and unbalanced forces, and that you can use scientific terms correctly.

The missing words in each sentence are opposites of one another. Choose the best words to complete each sentence. Choose from:

backward   balanced   downward   forward

slow down   speed up   unbalanced   upward

a   When the forces on an object are unbalanced, they can make it

    .... or ....

b   The blue car is not moving because the forces on it are

    ....

    The red car is starting to move because the forces on it are

    ....

c   The aeroplane stays at the same height above the ground because the force

    acting in the .... direction is equal and opposite to

    the force acting in the .... direction.

d   The spider moves at a constant speed because the ....

    force produced by its legs is equal and opposite to the

    .... force caused by friction.

Exercise 2 Comparatives

In this exercise about the effects of unbalanced forces, you practise using comparatives.

Look at **Comparative and superlative adjectives** in the *English skills and support* section for information about comparatives and superlatives.

Complete each sentence by using the words **greater** or **smaller.**

 a

The block begins to move forward because the force pushing forward

is .... than the force pushing backward.

b The train accelerates because the force of friction of its wheels on the rails

is .... than the forward force produced by its engine.

c The striped parachute has a larger surface area than the plain one, so the

air resistance on the striped parachute is ....

d To make the speed of the bicycle increase, the forward force must become

................., or air resistance and friction must become ....

e

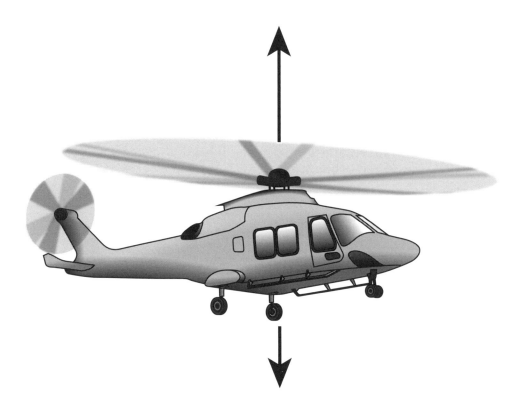

The helicopter begins to move upward when the upward force produced by

its rotors is .... than its weight.

> 3.2 Speed

Exercise 1 Connecting words

Connecting words help to link two parts of a sentence together. You are going to choose the one that makes the best sense in these sentences about speed.

Look at **Connecting words** in the *English skills and support* section for information about connecting words.

Choose the best connecting word to complete each sentence. Choose from the following words. You can use each word once, more than once or not at all.

and   because   but   so

a   You have measured the speed of the car in metres per second, ...
I asked you to measure it in kilometres per hour.

b   It is useful to calculate average speed .... the speed during a journey is not always constant.

c

The bee flies 100 m in 20 s, ... its average speed is 5 m/s.

d The speed of the cyclist was greater than the speed of the walker,

.... the cyclist arrived first.

e Marcus took 14.2 s to complete the race, ... Arun took
only 13.9 s.

Exercise 2 The more . . ., the more

In this exercise, you think hard about speed, distance and time. You also
practise using a sentence structure that we often use in science.

Complete each sentence. Choose from these words. Sometimes, there is more than
one word that works well in the sentence – just choose the one that feels best to you.

> **greater   faster   less   slower   smaller**

a The faster Marcus runs, the .... time he takes to finish the race.

b The greater the number of metres covered each second, the ....
the speed.

c The greater the time taken to cover 1 km, the .... the speed.

d The greater the difference between Sofia's and Zara's cycling speed, the

.... the difference in the distance they can cycle in 30 minutes.

e The smaller the distance the car has to travel, the .... time it
takes to arrive if it travels at an average speed of 45 km per hour.

> 3.3 Describing movement

Exercise 1 Graph vocabulary

In this exercise, you make sure that you can use some of the words needed for describing graphs.

Look at **Graphs** in the *English skills and support* section for information about graphs.

Draw lines from the words on the left to their meanings on the right.

Two of the words have the same meaning.

Words
distance/time graph
x-axis
y-axis
stationary
at rest
sketch
scale

Meanings
draw a graph without putting numbers on the axes
not moving
the numbers on the axis of a graph
the bottom (across) axis on a graph
a graph showing distance plotted against time
the side (up) axis on a graph

Exercise 2 Describing graphs

In this exercise, you check that you understand some of the words that we use when we talk about distance/time graphs.

Look at **Graphs** in the *English skills and support* section for information about graphs.

Arun walks to the shops. Here is the distance/time graph for his journey.

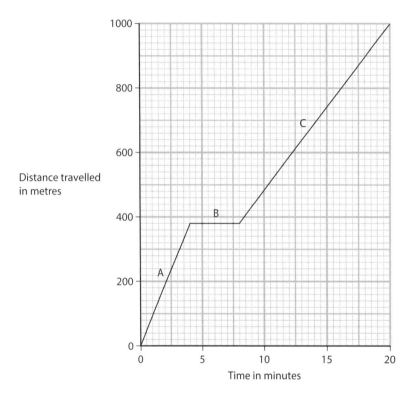

a   What is shown on the horizontal axis of the graph?

    ....

b   What is shown on the vertical axis of the graph?

    ....

c   What are the units used for measuring time on this graph?

    ....

d   What are the units used for measuring distance on this graph?

    ....

e   Which part or parts of the graph are straight lines? Write the letter(s) **A**, **B** and/or **C**.

    ....

f   Which part or parts of the graph are horizontal lines? Write the letter(s) **A**, **B** and/or **C**.

    ....

g   Which part or parts of the graph show when Arun is standing still?
    Write the letter(s) **A**, **B** and/or **C**.

    ....

h   Which part or parts of the graph show when Arun is walking at a constant speed? Write the letter(s) **A**, **B** and/or **C**.

    ....

> 3.4 Turning forces

Prepositions are small words, but it is easy to get them wrong. In this exercise, you choose the best one to complete sentences about turning forces.

Look at **Prepositions** in the *English skills and support* section for information about prepositions.

Exercise 1 Prepositions

Complete each sentence, using the best preposition. Choose from these prepositions.

down   from   for   of   on   up

a   Sofia needs to push harder .... the lever to lift the rock.

b   Marcus is heavier than Arun, so the seesaw tips .... on Marcus's side.

c   The masses are equal, but the mass on the left is further .... the pivot, so it produces a greater turning force.

d   A seesaw is a type .... lever.

e   Moment is another word .... turning force.

Exercise 2 Active and passive verbs

Sentences with active verbs are simpler than ones with passive verbs.
In this exercise, you practise using active verbs instead of passive ones.

Look at **Active and passive** in the *English skills and support* section for
information about active and passive verbs.

Each sentence contains a passive verb. Rewrite the sentence using an active verb.

For example:

(passive verb) The lever **is pushed** by Zara.

(active verb) Zara **pushes** the lever.

a   The door handle **is turned** by Marcus.

....

....

....

b   The turning effect **is produced** by Arun pressing on the lever.

....

....

....

c   The bicycle **is stopped** when Sofia turns the brake lever.

....

....

....

d

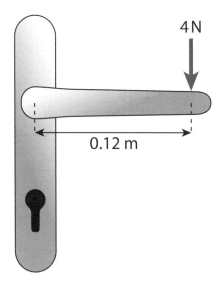

4 N

0.12 m

The value of the moment **is calculated** by multiplying force and distance.

....

....

....

e   The seesaw **is balanced** by putting a heavier weight on this end.

....

....

....

f   Turning forces **are measured** in newton metres.

....

....

....

> 3.5 Pressure between solids

Exercise 1 Vocabulary

This exercise provides practice in using some of the words we use to write about pressure.

Choose the best words to complete these sentences.

blunt   dividing   force   grams   moment

multiplying   newtons   pressure   sharp   surface area

a   The pushing effect of a force is called ....

b   We calculate pressure by .... the force by the .... on which it acts.

c   We measure pressure in .... per metre squared.

d   The pressure I can produce with a .... pin is greater than with a .... one.

e   If I stand on one leg, the .... I produce on the ground is greater than when I stand on two legs.

Exercise 2 Writing two or more sentences in an answer

Sometimes, a question needs a slightly longer answer than usual. In this exercise, you practise writing your own sentences to answer some 'Explain' questions.

Look at **Command words** in the *English skills and support* section for information about command words.

Write at least **two** sentences to answer each of these three questions. Make sure that your second sentence has some new information in it and is not just the first sentence written in a different way.

a   Explain why it is easier to cut an apple with a sharp knife than a blunt knife.

....

....

....

....

b   Explain what you need to know in order to calculate the pressure that an object is producing on the floor.

....

....

....

....

c   Explain why the large feet of a camel help to stop it sinking into sand.

....

....

....

....

> 3.6 Pressure in liquids and gases

Exercise 1 Putting words in the correct sequence

Each sentence has some words in the wrong place. Identify the mistakes, and rewrite the sentence correctly.

For example:

A gas produces a container on its pressure because its particles collide with the sides of the container.

A gas produces a pressure on its container because its particles collide with the sides of the container.

a   When you blow up a balloon, its volume colliding because there are more gas particles increases with the sides of the balloon.

   ....

   ....

b   The pressure on a submarine at sea level is higher than the pressure at great depth.

   ....

   ....

c   The less you go in the Earth's atmosphere, the higher the pressure.

   ....

   ....

d   Altitudes pressure decreases at higher atmospheric.

   ....

   ....

Exercise 2 Observations, results, conclusions and explanations

This exercise gives you practice in identifying observations, results and conclusions, and giving explanations.

Look at **The language of science experiments** in the *English skills and support* section for information about observations, results, conclusions and explanations.

Zara does an experiment to find out how pressure in a liquid changes with depth. She makes three holes in a bottle, and then fills it with liquid. The diagram shows what she sees.

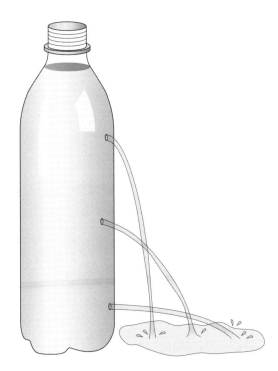

Zara measures the horizontal distance travelled by the water. She finds that the water from the top hole travels 4 cm from the side of the bottle, while the water from the middle and bottom holes travels 7 cm and 10 cm from the side.

a   What observations does Zara make?

   ....

   ....

   ....

b   What are the results of Zara's experiment?

   ....

   ....

   ....

c   What conclusion can Zara make from her experiment?

   ....

   ....

   ....

d   Write an explanation for Zara's results.

   ....

   ....

   ....

   ....

> 3.7 Particles on the move

It is important to do what the command word in a question asks you to do. In this exercise, you practise responding to three different command words.

Look at **Command words** in the *English skills and support* section for information about command words.

Exercise 1 Answering questions

Sofia carefully adds a drop of red ink to a beaker of water. The ink dissolves in the water.

a   **Describe** what Sofia will see over the next few minutes.

....

....

....

b   **Name** the process that happens in the beaker.

....

c   **Explain** how the red colour spreads through the water.

....

....

....

....

Exercise 2 Modal verbs

Modal verbs tell us about certainties and possibilities. In this exercise, you think about diffusion and practise using modal verbs.

Look at **Modal verbs** in the *English skills and support* section for information about modal verbs.

Choose the best word or words to complete each sentence. Choose from these words.

might   **might not**   **should**   **should not**

a   If it is colder, the colour ………….....………….. diffuse as quickly as usual.

b   If you want to slow down the rate of diffusion, you …………...…..……… heat the liquid.

c   If you want to stop the scent of the perfume spreading around the room, you

    …………….....……… keep the lid on the bottle.

d   If the concentration of the gas is almost the same in the two parts of the

    room, diffusion …………...…..……… happen very quickly.

e   If you want to find out how increasing the temperature affects the rate of

    diffusion, you ………....…...……… keep everything the same except

    temperature.

4 Ecosystems

> 4.1 The Sonoran Desert

Exercise 1 Vocabulary

> This exercise checks that you understand some of the new words in this topic.

Choose the word that matches each description. Choose from these words. You do not need to use all of them.

> adaptations   cacti   cactuses   ecology   ecosystem
>
> habitat   interactions   nectar   nocturnal   pollination

a   being active at night rather than in the daytime ....

b   transferring pollen from one flower to another ....

c   a sweet substance produced in flowers, to attract insects ....

d   features of an organism that help it to survive in its environment

....

e   the network of interactions between all the living and non-living things in a

particular place ....

f   the study of living organisms in their environment ....

g   the place where an organism lives ....

h   the plural of cactus ....

Exercise 2 Singular and plural verbs

> This exercise is about choosing the correct form of a verb to complete a
> sentence about ecosystems.

Look at **Singular and plural verbs** in the *English skills and support* section
for information about singular and plural verbs.

<u>Underline</u> the correct verb in each sentence.

a   An arrow in a food web **represent** / **represents** the transfer of energy.

b   The animals and plants in a desert **interact** / **interacts** in many different ways.

c   Kangaroo rats are nocturnal, so they **look** / **looks** for food at night.

d   A cactus **is** / **are** adapted to live in dry places.

e   Not all of the interactions between organisms in an ecosystem **involve** /
      involves food webs.

> 4.2 Different ecosystems

Exercise 1 Completing sentences

> In this exercise, you will complete some sentences without being provided
> with words to choose from. Instead, you are just given the first letter.

Choose suitable words to complete these paragraphs about two ecosystems.
It's a good idea to read the whole paragraph first, as this might help you to
think of suitable words to fill the spaces.

The Arctic Ocean is covered with i.................. in the winter. This provides a surface

on which foxes and polar bears can hunt for s.................. , which have to come to

the surface to breathe a........................ .

Mangrove trees grow in sea w.................................... , along the coasts of many

t............................ countries. Their leaves fall into the mud, and provide

f....................... for prawns and crabs.

Exercise 2 Active and passive verbs

In this exercise, you practise using active verbs instead of passive ones.

Look at **Active and passive** in the *English skills and support* section for information about active and passive verbs.

Each sentence contains a passive verb. Rewrite the sentence using an active verb. Sometimes, you will need to choose a subject for the sentence – for example 'you' or 'we'.

For example:

(passive) The traps are checked regularly.

(active) We check the traps regularly.

a

A pitfall trap can be used by Sofia to catch beetles.

....

....

b   A book can be used by Marcus to identify these plants.

....

....

c   A good habitat for mud skippers is provided by mangroves.

....

....

d   Risks can be reduced by always working with a partner.

....

....

e   A photograph is taken to record the appearance of the plants.

....

....

> 4.3 Intruders in an ecosystem

Exercise 1 Modal verbs

In this exercise, you think about the effects that an introduced species might have, and choose the best word to complete each sentence.

Look at **Modal verbs** in the *English skills and support* section for information about modal verbs.

Complete the sentences, using the words in the list. You can use each word once, more than once or not at all.

can   cannot   might   might not   should   should not

a   Species from one country .... be introduced into another

   country, because they .... harm the native species.

b   Although everyone agrees that this introduced species is harming our native

   species, some people .... be happy for it to be killed.

c   If the introduced species is a predator, it .... eat the eggs of
   the native birds.

d   Introduced species .... be eradicated easily.

e   An introduced species .... cause some of the native species
   to become extinct.

Exercise 2 Prepositions

In this exercise, you choose the best preposition to complete sentences about introduced species.

Look at **Prepositions** in the *English skills and support* section for information about prepositions.

Complete each sentence, using the best preposition. Choose from these prepositions. You can use each one once, more than once or not at all.

between   **by**   **from**   **in**   **on**   **to**

a   When stoats were introduced .... New Zealand, they reduced the populations of native birds.

b   Many species have been made extinct .... humans.

c   An introduced plant might be better than the native plants at obtaining minerals .... the soil.

d   An introduced species can disrupt the interactions .... the organisms in the ecosystem.

e   Many of the native species of birds in New Zealand nest .... the ground.

> 4.4 Bioaccumulation

Exercise 1 Positive or negative?

In this exercise, you choose whether a positive or negative statement about bioaccumulation is correct.

<u>Underline</u> the correct choice in each statement.

a   Bioaccumulation **means** / **does not mean** the increase in concentration of a substance as you go up a food chain.

b   Biomagnification **means** / **does not mean** the build-up of a substance in an organism's body.

c   Persistent insecticides **do** / **do not** break down easily.

d   **All** / **not all** insecticides are persistent.

e   **All** / **not all** insectides are biodegradable.

Exercise 2 The more . . ., the more

In this exercise, you think about bioaccumulation. You also practise using a sentence structure that we often use in science.

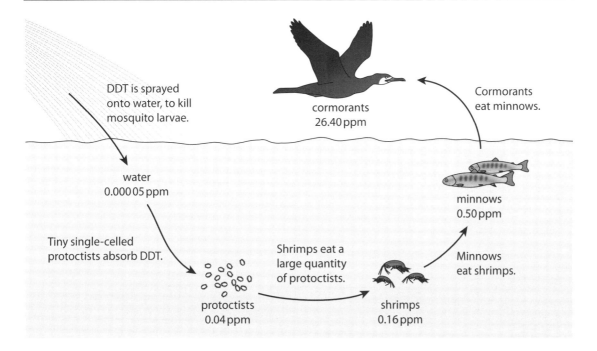

Choose the best word to complete each sentence.

a   The harder it is for an insectide to break down, the .... it will accumulate in the bodies of organisms.

b   The further you go along a food chain, the .... the concentration of DDT in an organism's body.

c   The longer the lifetime of an animal, the .... the quantity of the persistent insecticide it will accumulate.

d   The more DDT is used, the .... the danger that birds of prey will die out.

e   The more toxic a substance is, the .... likely it is that organisms will survive being sprayed with it.

5 > Materials and cycles on Earth

> 5.1 The structure of the atom

Exercise 1 Connecting words

In this exercise, you use suitable connecting words to complete descriptions of the structure of an atom.

Look at **Connecting words** in the *English skills and support* section for information about connecting words.

Choose the best words to complete the sentences.

and   because   but   but not

a   We cannot see atoms ……………… they are so small.

b   The nucleus of an atom contains neutrons ……………… electrons.

c   A proton ……………… a neutron have the same mass.

d   Electrons, neutrons ……………… protons are subatomic particles.

e   Electrons have a negative charge ……………… protons have a positive charge.

Exercise 2 Answering questions

It is important to do what the command word in a question asks you to do. In this exercise, you practise responding to three different command words.

Look at **Command words** in the *English skills and support* section for information about command words.

a **Name** the negatively charged particles in an atom.

....

b **Describe** the three types of subatomic particle in an atom.

....

....

....

....

....

....

c **Explain** why an atom has no overall charge.

....

....

....

....

....

....

> 5.2 Purity

Exercise 1 Singular and plural verbs

This exercise is about choosing the correct form of a verb to complete a sentence about purity.

Look at **Singular and plural verbs** in the *English skills and support* section for information about singular and plural verbs.

<u>Underline</u> the correct verb in each sentence.

a   The reaction between silver nitrate and sodium chloride **does not / do not** produce pure silver chloride.

b   The water in all of these bottles **is / are** pure.

c   Marcus **wears / wear** safety glasses when doing chemistry experiments.

d   About 68% of salt in seawater **is / are** sodium chloride.

e   All pure diamonds **is / are** translucent.

Exercise 2 Putting words in the correct sequence

In this exercise, you use your understanding of purity to sort out some mixed up sentences.

In each sentence, two words need to swap places.
Write the corrected sentences.

For example:

Any gold does not contain pure silver or copper.

Pure gold does not contain any silver or copper.

a   In some product reactions, only one chemical is formed.

....

....

b   Universal indicator can tell us when the product has formed a neutral reaction.

....

....

c   The reactions between some mixtures produce impure substances of products.

....

....

d   All elements are mixtures of two or more alloys, so they are not pure.

....

....

> 5.3 Weather and climate

Exercise 1 Weather and climate vocabulary

In this exercise, you make sure that you can use some of the words needed for writing about weather and climate.

Draw lines from the words on the left to their meanings on the right.

Words	Meanings
weather	the study of weather
atmosphere	the average yearly patterns of temperature, rainfall etc.
humidity	how far it is possible to see
visibility	numerical data that we can use to work out, for example, the climate of a place
climate	how much water vapour is present in the atmosphere
statistics	the temperature, rainfall etc. today or this week
meteorology	the air around us; the gases that surround a planet
climatology	the study of climate

Exercise 2 Writing two or more sentences in an answer

Sometimes, a question needs a slightly longer answer than usual.
In this exercise, you practise writing your own sentences to answer
some 'Describe' and 'Explain' questions.

Look at **Command words** in the *English skills and support* section for
information about command words.

Write at least **two** sentences to answer each of these three questions. Make sure
that your second sentence has some new information in it and is not just the first
sentence written in a different way.

Make sure that you do what the command word says.

a   Explain the difference between climate and weather.

....

....

....

....

b   Describe what the weather is like at your school today.

....

....

....

....

c   Explain why temperature readings are usually taken in the shade.

....

....

....

....

› 5.4 Climate and ice ages

Exercise 1 Completing sentences

In this exercise, you will complete some sentences without being provided with words to choose from.

Choose suitable words to complete these paragraphs about climate and ice ages. It is a good idea to read the whole paragraph first, as this might help you to think of suitable words to fill the spaces.

There is ice at both the North Pole and South Pole today, so we know that the Earth

is in an .... However, the ice only covers the land quite

close to the poles, so we are in an interglacial period and not in a .... period.

Over the last 2 billion years, there have been several ice ages. In each ice age, the

climate has .... between glacial and interglacial periods. Boulders that

have been left behind by .... provide evidence that the climate was

much colder in the past.

Exercise 2 Observations, conclusions and explanations

This exercise gives you practice in identifying observations and conclusions, and giving explanations.

Look at **The language of science experiments** in the *English skills and support* section for information about observations, conclusions and explanations.

A researcher extracted a core of peat from a very old peat bog. She found that the peat from the deepest part of the core contained pollen grains from plants that are adapted to living in cold places. Nearer the top of the core, the pollen grains were from plants that can only live in warmer places.

a   What observations did the researcher make?

....

....

....

b   What conclusion can the researcher make from her observations?

....

....

c   Explain how the researcher's observations can lead to this conclusion.

....

....

....

....

> 5.5 Atmosphere and climate

Exercise 1 Vocabulary

This exercise helps you to check that you understand the new terms used in this topic.

Choose the word from the list that best matches each description. Take care to copy the word exactly, without making any spelling mistakes.

biodegradable   bioplastics   deforestation   emissions   fossil fuels

global warming   locked up   photosynthesis   recycled   renewable resource

a   can be broken down by decomposers ....

b   an increase in the average temperatures on Earth ....

c   plastics made from waste biomass ....

d   cutting down large quantities of trees ....

e   something that is replaced after we have used it, so that there is always more

to use ....

f   substances made from semi-decayed organisms millions of years ago, which

we can use as an energy source ....

g   waste gases or liquids that are released from, for example, cars or factories

....

h   a process in which plants take carbon dioxide from the atmosphere

....

i   stored away, so that it cannot escape easily ....

j   used again ....

Exercise 2 Writing sentences about an analogy

> We use analogies to help us to understand a structure or a process. An analogy compares the structure or process to something familiar. In this exercise, you practise writing complete sentences.

The way that a blanket keeps us warm can be used as an analogy to help us to think about how carbon dioxide in the atmosphere affects the temperature of the Earth.

We can also use the warming effect of glass in a greenhouse as an analogy for the warming effect of carbon dioxide in the Earth's atmosphere.

a   Describe how carbon dioxide in the atmosphere is similar to a blanket.

....

....

....

....

b   Describe how carbon dioxide in the atmosphere differs from a blanket.

....

....

....

....

c   Describe how the effect of carbon dioxide in the atmosphere is similar to the effect of glass in a greenhouse.

....

....

....

....

6 ▶ Light

> 6.1 Reflection

Exercise 1 Prepositions

When you write about reflection, it is important to use the correct preposition. You will practise that in this exercise.

Look at **Prepositions** in the *English skills and support* section for information about prepositions.

The diagram shows a plane mirror, an incident light ray and a reflected light ray.

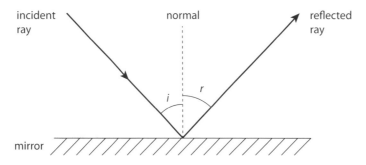

Choose the correct preposition to complete each sentence about the diagram.

Draw ~~a line through~~ the incorrect preposition in each sentence.

a   The incident ray reflects **at / to** the surface of the mirror.

b   The incident ray goes **by / onto** the mirror.

c   The reflected ray comes **from / to** the mirror.

d   The mirror reflects the incident ray **from / by** its surface

e   The reflected ray travels **onto / from** the surface of the mirror.

f   The normal is perpendicular **at / to** the surface of the mirror.

Exercise 2 Investigating reflection

When you plan an experiment, you need to think about variables. In this exercise, you check that you know the correct words for the different kinds of variables in an investigation and also think about the names of the apparatus that you use.

Zara and Sofia want to investigate the law of reflection. They want to find out if the angle of reflection always equals the angle of incidence.

This is the apparatus that they use.

They choose the angle of incidence, and then draw the incident ray, normal and reflected ray, like this.

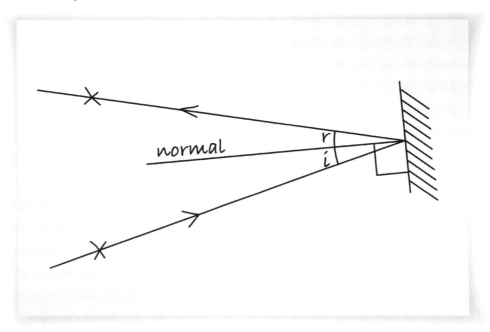

They measure the angles labelled *r* and *i*. Then they repeat this process, with a different angle of incidence.

a What is the **independent variable** in the girls' investigation?
Tick (✔) the correct answer.

the angle of incidence ☐

the angle of reflection ☐

the length of the normal ☐

the size of the mirror ☐

b What is the **dependent variable** in their investigation? Tick (✔) the correct answer.

the angle of incidence ☐

the angle of reflection ☐

the length of the normal ☐

the size of the mirror ☐

c What is the name for the type of diagram that the girls draw?

....

d Which apparatus do the girls use to draw the normal? Tick (✓) **all** the correct boxes.

pencil ☐

ruler ☐

set square ☐

e Name the apparatus that the girls use to measure the angle of incidence and the angle of reflection.

....

› 6.2 Refraction

Exercise 1 Refraction vocabulary

> In this exercise, you complete sentences using some of the vocabulary you have learnt in this topic.

Choose suitable words to complete these paragraphs about refraction. Choose from the list. You can use each word once, more than once or not at all.

angle of incidence   **angle of refraction**   **away**   **equal**   **from**

normal   **reflected**   **refracted**   **right**   **towards**

The diagram shows a light ray passing from the air into a glass block.

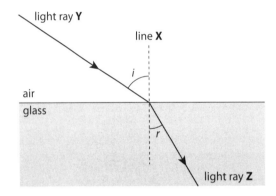

When the incident ray hits the surface of the glass block, it is ....

The light ray is bent .... line X. Line X is the ....

Line X is drawn at a .... angle to the surface of the glass block.

Angle *i* is the .... and angle *r* is the ....

Exercise 2 Correcting statements about refraction

This exercise gives you practice in writing sentences about refraction.

Each statement is incorrect. Rewrite the statement so that it is correct.

a   When light passes from air into water, it speeds up.

....

b   When light passes from air into water, it is bent away from the normal.

....

c   When light passes from one medium to another, it always bends towards the normal.

....

....

d   Lenses in glasses (spectacles) work by reflecting light rays.

....

e   The angle of incidence is the angle between the incident ray and the surface of the glass block.

....

....

> 6.3 Making rainbows

Exercise 1 Vocabulary check

This exercise will help you to check that you understand the new vocabulary you have learnt in this topic.

The diagram shows dispersion of a ray of light.

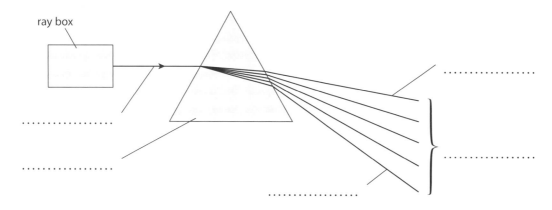

a Write in the missing labels for the diagram. Use these words.

   blue light   **prism**   **red light**   **spectrum**   **white light**

b On the diagram, write the letter **D** to show where **dispersion** happens.

Exercise 2 Putting words in the correct sequence

In this exercise, you use your understanding of dispersion of light to sort out some mixed up sentences.

In each sentence, two words are in the wrong place.

Rewrite the sentences correctly, by swapping two words in each one.

For example:

Raindrops form when white light is dispersed through rainbows.

Rainbows form when white light is dispersed through raindrops.

a   Light is refracted at a mirror, and reflected when it passes into a triangular prism.

   ....

   ....

b   As white light passes through a prism, red light is refracted more than blue light.

   ....

   ....

c   Refraction happens because dispersion of some colours of light is greater than others.

   ....

   ....

d   The spectrum of colours we see when white light is dispersed is called a range.

   ....

   ....

> 6.4 Colours of light

Exercise 1 Vocabulary check

In this exercise, you make sure that you can correctly use some of the words needed for writing about colours of light.

Draw lines from the words on the left to their meanings on the right.

Words	Meanings
cyan	the three colours of light from which all other colours can be made
primary colours	a colour of light made by mixing red light and blue light
white	a colour of light made by mixing blue light and green light
magenta	a transparent object that lets some colours of light pass through, but not others
yellow	light produced by mixing all the primary colours
coloured filter	a colour of light made by mixing green light and red light

Exercise 2 Writing about colours of light

In this exercise, you check that you understand colours of light by selecting the best words to complete sentences.

Choose the correct word to complete each sentence. ~~Draw a line through~~ the incorrect word.

a A green filter absorbs all colours of light except **green / red**.

b A green filter transmits only **red / green** light.

c All the colours except **blue / green** are subtracted as light passes through a green filter.

d When green light shines on a red filter, **no / red** light will pass through.

e A yellow book looks yellow because it **absorbs / reflects** yellow light.

f A red book looks **black / blue** when we shine blue light onto it.

› 6.5 Galaxies

Exercise 1 Answering questions

It is important to do what the command word in a question asks you to do. In this exercise, you practise responding to three different command words.

Look *at* **Command words** in the *English skills and support* section for information about command words.

a   **Name** the force that holds together the stars, dust and solar systems in our galaxy.

....

b   **Describe** the shape of our galaxy.

....

....

c   **Explain** why we see our galaxy, the Milky Way, as a band of stars across the sky.

....

....

....

....

Exercise 2 Modal verbs

In this exercise, you think about galaxies, and choose the best word to complete each sentence.

Look at **Modal verbs** in the *English skills and support* section for information about modal verbs.

Choose the best word to complete each sentence. Choose from the list.

can   **cannot**   **might**   **might not**

a   Galaxies .... be spiral, elliptical or irregular.

b   We .... count the number of stars in our galaxy exactly.

c   We .... use the word space to mean the whole of the universe and everything in it.

d   Scientists estimate that there .... be 100 000 000 000 galaxies in the universe.

e   It .... take an astronaut 100 000 years to travel across our galaxy.

> 6.6 Rocks in space

Exercise 1 Comparatives and superlatives

In this exercise about asteroids, you practise using comparatives and superlatives.

Look at **Comparative and superlative adjectives** in the *English skills and support* section for information about comparatives and superlatives.

Choose a suitable comparative or superlative word to complete each sentence. Choose from these words.

>   larger   largest   smaller   smallest

a   An asteroid is .... than a planet.

b   The force of gravity on an asteroid is .... than the force of gravity on Venus.

c   The number of asteroids in the Solar System is .... than the number of planets.

d   This tiny asteroid is one of the .... objects in the Solar System.

e   The chance of a small asteroid hitting Earth is .... than the chance of a large asteroid hitting Earth.

f   The deepest craters are made by the impacts of the .... asteroids.

g   The .... number of asteroids is found in the asteroid belt.

Exercise 2 Active and passive verbs

Sentences with active verbs are simpler than ones with passive verbs.
In this exercise, you practise using active verbs instead of passive ones.

Look at **Active and passive** in the *English skills and support* section for information about active and passive verbs.

Each sentence contains a passive verb. Rewrite the sentence using an active verb.

a   The Sun **is orbited** by asteroids and planets.

   ....

   ....

b   Only a weak force of gravity **is produced** by small asteroids.

   ....

   ....

c   The craters **were produced** by the impacts of asteroids.

   ....

   ....

d   Asteroids **were formed** from rocks left over from the formation of the
   Solar System.

   ....

   ....

e   The asteroid 2019 LF6 **was discovered** by astronomers in 2019.

   ....

   ....

7 ▸ Diet and growth

⟩ 7.1 Nutrients

Exercise 1 Vocabulary

In this exercise, you check that you remember the new vocabulary you have learnt in this topic.

Choose the word from the list that best matches each description. Use each word once only. Take care to copy the word exactly, without making any spelling mistakes.

anaemia   carbohydrate   fats   minerals
oil   protein   vitamins

a   a nutrient that helps us to produce new cells, for growth and repair

....

b   two nutrients that we use to provide energy

.... and ....

c   an illness that can be caused by a lack of iron in the diet ....

d   a type of fat that is liquid at room temperature ....

e   nutrients that we require in only small quantities in our diet; they include

A, C and D ....

f   iron and calcium are examples of this group of nutrients ....

Exercise 2 Singular and plural verbs

This exercise is about choosing the correct form of a verb to complete a sentence about nutrients.

Look at **Singular and plural verbs** in the *English skills and support* section for information about singular and plural verbs.

<u>Underline</u> the correct verb in each sentence.

a   There **is / are** several types of nutrient that we should eat each day.

b   Starch **is / are** a type of carbohydrate.

c   Both iron and calcium **is / are** important components of our diet.

d   Carbohydrate and fat **provide / provides** us with energy.

e   Fat stores beneath the skin **provide / provides** insulation.

> 7.2 A balanced diet

Exercise 1 Describing a bar chart

This exercise helps you to check that you understand the vocabulary used for graphs and bar charts, and that you can write a sentence to provide a clear explanation.

Look at **Graphs** in the *English skills and support* section for information about graphs.

The bar chart shows how much energy different people need each day.

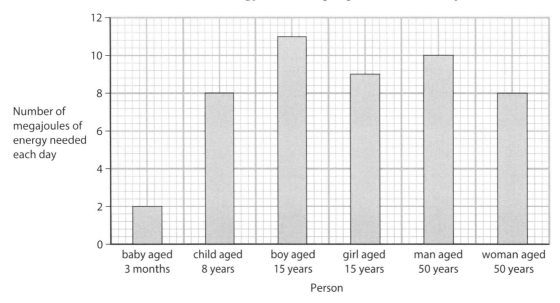

a   What is shown on the horizontal axis of the bar chart?

   ....

b   What is shown on the vertical axis of the bar chart?

   ....

c   What are the units in which energy is measured on the bar chart?

   ....

d What is the range of the scale on the vertical axis?

....

e Explain why the bars on this bar chart are drawn so that they do not touch each other.

....

....

....

Exercise 2 Writing sentences

In this exercise, you practise writing complete sentences without any help.

Complete each of these sentences. Make sure that you include useful information about diet in each of your sentences. For example, when you are writing about a balanced diet, you could include the names of the nutrients that should be included in a balanced diet. Try to spell each word correctly.

a A balanced diet ....

....

....

b Constipation ....

....

....

c Fats from animals ....

....

....

d   Fibre ....

....

....

e   Young children ....

....

....

> 7.3 Growth, development and health

Exercise 1 Using comparatives and superlatives

In this exercise, you can make your own choice of comparatives to describe differences, and then answer some questions that use superlatives.

Look at **Comparative and superlative adjectives** in the *English skills and support* section for information about comparatives and superlatives.

The picture shows three members of the same family – a toddler (small child), boy and man.

Complete these sentences by using a comparative word.

a   The toddler is .... than the child.

b   The child has .... legs than the toddler.

c   The man is .... and ....
than the child and toddler.

Answer these questions.

d Who is the tallest?

....

e Who is the youngest?

....

f Who is the oldest?

....

Exercise 2 Completing sentences

This exercise tests your understanding of some of the vocabulary you have met in this topic.

Use words from the list to complete the sentences. You need to use each word once. There is one word in the list that you do not need to use.

carbon dioxide   carbon monoxide   development   embryo

nicotine   oxygen   particulates   tar

Smoking cigarettes can damage health. If a pregnant woman smokes, she can harm

the .... of the .... as well as damage her

own health.

Cigarettes contain a substance called .... , which is addictive.

Cigarette smoke also contains tiny pieces of carbon, called .... ,

which get into the smoker's lungs and damage the alveoli. The gas

.... is also found in cigarette smoke, and this reduces the ability of

the blood to transport .... The .... in

cigarette smoke increases the risk of developing cancer.

› 7.4 Moving the body

Exercise 1 Prepositions

When you write about muscles and what they do, it is important to use the correct preposition. You will practise that in this exercise.

Look at **Prepositions** in the *English skills and support* section for information about prepositions.

The diagram shows some of the bones and muscles in the arm.

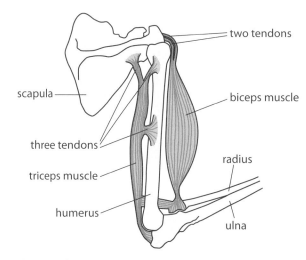

Choose the best preposition in the list to complete each sentence about the diagram. You can use each word once, more than once or not at all.

along   at   by   from   on   to

a   The biceps muscle is attached .... the radius.

b   When the triceps muscle contracts, it pulls .... the ulna.

c   When you want to bend your arm, the brain sends an electrical impulse ....
     a neurone to the biceps muscle.

d   A muscle can generate a force .... contracting.

e   The ulna and humerus meet .... the elbow joint.

f   When a muscle contracts, it pulls .... the tendon that attaches it

     .... a bone.

Exercise 2 Connecting words

We use connecting words to connect two ideas in a sentence.

Look at **Connecting words** in the *English skills and support* section for information about connecting words.

We use 'but' to connect two contrasting ideas, and 'and' to connect two similar ideas. Complete each sentence using either **and** or **but**.

a   Insects have an exoskeleton .... vertebrates have a skeleton inside their body.

b   Hinge joints .... ball-and-socket joints allow bones to move.

c   Hinge joints allow movement in one plane .... ball-and-socket joints allow movement in a complete circle.

d   The skeleton of the arms and shoulders includes hinge joints .... ball-and-socket joints.

e   Muscles can pull .... not push.

f   The biceps is attached to the bones in the upper arm and shoulder by two tendons .... the triceps is attached by three tendons.

8 ▶ Chemical reactions

> 8.1 Exothermic reactions

Exercise 1 Verbs with 'out'

When we put a preposition after a verb, we usually change its meaning. This exercise gives you practice in using different verbs followed by 'out'.

Look at **Phrasal verbs** in the *English skills and support* section for information about phrasal verbs.

Choose the best verb to complete each sentence. Choose from the list. Use each verb at least once.

carry out	find out	give out	run out	spread out

a   Combustion reactions .... heat.

b   The reaction will stop when all the reactants ....

c   The gases produced in this reaction have .... into the air.

d   I want to .... if this reaction involves oxidation.

e   The boys .... an investigation to discover which fuel produces the greatest temperature rise.

f   Dissipate means to ....

Exercise 2 Planning and doing an experiment

This exercise checks that you understand some of the vocabulary that we use when planning experiments.

Sofia and Marcus investigate the exothermic reaction between magnesium ribbon and hydrochloric acid. They do an experiment to test this hypothesis:

The greater the mass of magnesium ribbon, the greater the temperature increase.

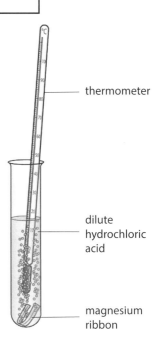

thermometer

dilute hydrochloric acid

magnesium ribbon

a   Before Sofia and Marcus do their experiment, they try using different masses of magnesium ribbon and different volumes of hydrochloric acid, to check that they can measure the temperature change.

What do we call this work that you do, before starting the main experiment?

....

b   What is the independent variable in Sofia and Marcus's experiment?

....

c   What is the dependent variable in their experiment?

....

d   State **two** variables that they should keep the same.

....

....

e   Name the measuring instrument that they use to measure the change in temperature.

....

f   State the units that they use to measure the temperature change.

....

› 8.2 Endothermic reactions

Exercise 1 Describing differences

Describing the difference between two terms is a good way of checking that you understand their meanings.

Write a sentence to describe the difference between each of the pairs of words.

Use the word 'but' to connect the two halves of your sentence.

Here is an example:

independent variable and dependent variable:

The independent variable is the one that you change in an experiment, but the dependent variable is the one that you measure when you collect your results.

a   exothermic and endothermic

....

....

....

b   accurate and precise

....

....

....

c   reactants and products

....

....

....

Exercise 2 Results and conclusions

This exercise is about the words and phrases we use to describe results charts and to complete them. It is also about the difference between a result and a conclusion.

Look at **The language of science experiments** in the *English skills and support* section for information about results and conclusions.

Zara investigates exothermic and endothermic reactions.

She places five different liquids into five test tubes. She measures the temperature of each liquid.

Then she adds a different substance to each liquid. She measures the temperature again after one minute.

Here are her results.

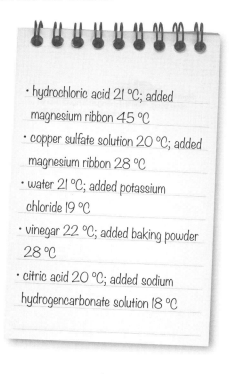

- hydrochloric acid 21 °C; added magnesium ribbon 45 °C
- copper sulfate solution 20 °C; added magnesium ribbon 28 °C
- water 21 °C; added potassium chloride 19 °C
- vinegar 22 °C; added baking powder 28 °C
- citric acid 20 °C; added sodium hydrogencarbonate solution 18 °C

This is the results chart that Zara drew.

Liquid	Substance added to liquid	Initial temperature	Final temperature	Change in temperature	Exothermic or endothermic?
hydrochloric acid	magnesium ribbon	21	45	+24	exothermic

a   Complete the headings of the third, fourth and fifth columns in Zara's table, by writing the units.

b   Which column shows Zara's **conclusions**?

   ....

c   Use Zara's results to complete the results chart. Take care to copy the words correctly and not make any spelling mistakes.

> 8.3 Reactions of metals with oxygen

Exercise 1 Connecting words

In this exercise, you check your understanding of the properties of metals by choosing suitable connecting words.

Look at **Connecting words** in the *English skills and support* section for information about connecting words.

Complete the sentences about metals, using **and**, **because**, **but** or **so**.

Lithium, sodium .... potassium are metals. They each have a dull

surface, ... look shiny when they are cut. The shiny surface goes dull

after a while .... the metal reacts with oxygen in the air.

These three metals react quickly with oxygen, ... iron reacts more

slowly .... it is a less reactive metal. Gold does not react with oxygen

at all, ... we say that it is inert.

Exercise 2 Modal verbs

This exercise asks you to complete sentences about metals reacting with oxygen, using the best modal verb.

Look at **Modal verbs** in the *English skills and support* section for information about modal verbs.

Choose the best modal verb to complete each sentence about metals reacting with oxygen. Choose from these words.

can   must

a   We .... prevent iron from rusting by painting it.

b   A scientist .... use gloves to handle sodium, because it would react with water on her hands.

c   If he uses tongs, Marcus .... heat the piece of metal safely.

d   We .... see that magnesium reacts more quickly than iron.

e   Sodium and potassium are so reactive that they .... be stored under oil.

> 8.4 Reactions of metals with water

Exercise 1 Comparatives and superlatives

In this exercise, you use comparatives and superlatives to describe the results of an experiment.

Look at **Comparative and superlative adjectives** in the *English skills and support* section for information about comparatives and superlatives.

Sofia and Zara investigate the reactivity of metals with water.

The table shows their results.

Metal	Observation when added to cold water	Observation when added to warm water
A	no reaction	a few bubbles
B	many bubbles	many bubbles produced very quickly
C	one or two bubbles	several bubbles
D	no reaction	no reaction

a   Which metal is the **most** reactive? ....

b   Which metal is the **least** reactive? ....

c   Which metals are **more** reactive than metal **A**? ....

d   Which metals are **less** reactive than metal **C**? ....

e   Write the letters of the metals in their order of reactivity, most reactive first.

     ....

Exercise 2 Making predictions

In this exercise, you are given some information, and then asked to make a prediction using the information and your own understanding of how metals react with water.

a   Gold is an inert metal.

Predict how gold will react with water.

....

....

b   Sodium is more reactive than calcium. Calcium reacts steadily with water.

Predict how sodium will react with water.

....

....

c   When a metal reacts with water, hydrogen gas is produced.

Predict what will happen if you put a lighted splint into the mouth of the test tube.

....

....

d   Some metals react with oxygen in the air, which produces a layer of metal oxide on the surface of the metal.

Predict how rubbing the surface of the metal with sandpaper will affect how the metal reacts with water.

....

....

> 8.5 Reactions of metals with dilute acids

Exercise 1 Writing word equations

In a word equation, we use words, + signs and arrows to show what happens in a chemical reaction. In this exercise, you use your understanding of chemical reactions to help you to choose the correct word to complete each equation.

Remember that no new kinds of atoms are formed in a chemical reaction. They are just rearranged into different combinations.

Complete these word equations to show what happens when metals react with dilute acids.

Choose from the list. You can use each word once, more than once or not at all.

chloride   **hydrochloric**   **hydrogen**

sulfide   **sulfuric**   **zinc**

a   magnesium + hydrochloric acid ⟶ magnesium .... + hydrogen

b   magnesium + ... acid ⟶ magnesium sulfate + hydrogen

c   zinc + ... acid ⟶ zinc chloride + ...

d   .... + sulfuric acid ⟶ zinc .... + hydrogen

e   lead + ... ⟶ lead sulfate + hydrogen

Exercise 2 Chemistry vocabulary

This exercise checks that you can use some of the new terms you have learnt in this topic, as well as a few from earlier chemistry topics.

Which word is being described? Choose from the list. Use each word once.

inert   **pure**   **reaction**

reactivity   **reagents**   **salt**

a   the chemicals that we use in an experiment ....

b   how easily and quickly a metal reacts ....

c   a substance such as zinc chloride, which is produced when a metal reacts

with a dilute acid ....

d   an event in which reactants are changed into products ....

e   an adjective used to describe a substance that is generally unreactive

....

f   an adjective used to describe a single substance, with no other substances

mixed with it ....

9 ▶ Magnetism

› 9.1 Magnetic fields

Exercise 1 The more . . ., the more

This exercise tests your understanding of magnets and magnetic fields.

Choose one of these words to complete each sentence.

stronger   **weaker**

a   The .... the magnet, the further its magnetic field extends.

b   The further apart the lines of its magnetic field, the ....
the magnet.

c   The stronger the magnet, the .... magnetic force it produces.

d   The closer to the poles of a magnet, the .... the magnetic force.

Exercise 2 Prepositions

This exercise asks you to choose the correct preposition to complete sentences about magnetic fields.

Look at **Prepositions** in the *English skills and support* section for information about prepositions.

The diagrams show the magnetic fields when two magnets are placed close to one another.

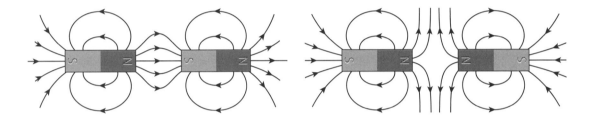

Choose the best preposition to complete each sentence about magnetic fields.

> **between**   **from**   **in**   **of**

a   The field lines .... a north pole and a south pole all point

.... the same direction.

b   There is a force .... attraction .... the north pole
of one magnet and the south pole of another magnet.

c   The magnetic field lines between two south poles point away ....
each other.

d   The field lines .... two like poles show why the magnets repel
each other.

e   The needle .... a compass turns to point ....

the direction .... the magnetic field.

> 9.2 The Earth as a giant magnet

Exercise 1 Answering questions

It is important to do what the command word in a question asks you to do. In this exercise, you practise responding to three different command words.

Look at **Command words** in the *English skills and support* section for information about command words.

The diagram shows the Earth's magnetic field.

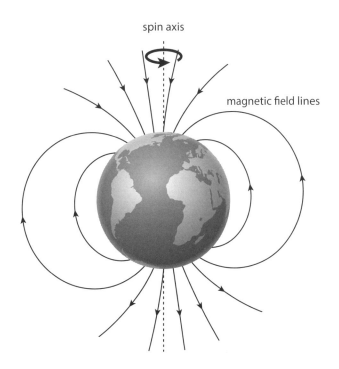

a **Name** the equipment we can use to help us to navigate by using the Earth's magnetic field.

....

b **Describe** the shape of the Earth's magnetic field.

....

....

....

c **Explain** the difference between geographic north and magnetic north.

....

....

....

....

Exercise 2 Putting words in the correct sequence

In this exercise, you use your understanding of the Earth's magnetic field to sort out some mixed up sentences.

In each sentence, two words are in the wrong place.

Rewrite the sentences correctly, by swapping two words in each one.

For example:

Rock is a naturally occurring magnetic magnetite.

Magnetite is a naturally occurring magnetic rock.

a   The axis on which the Earth passes spins through the geographic North and South Poles.

   ....

   ....

b   We think that the Earth has a liquid field because its outer core is made of magnetic iron.

   ....

   ....

c   If you have a direction, you can always find out in which compass you are facing.

   ....

   ....

d   Although we now have compasses to help us to navigate, ships and aeroplanes still use magnetic satellites.

   ....

   ....

> 9.3 Electromagnets

Exercise 1 Different forms of the same word

In this exercise, you complete sentences by selecting the correct form of words about magnets.

Use the correct words to complete each sentence. Choose from these words. You may not need to use all the words.

magnet　　**magnetic**　　**magnetise**

magnetised　　**magnetism**

a　We can .... a piece of soft iron by stroking it with a bar

　..................... .

b　A material that is attracted to a .... is said to be ....

c　We can make an electromagnet by wrapping a wire around a ....

　material and passing a current through the wire.

d　An electromagnet is not a permanent ....

e　When the current through the coil of an electromagnet is switched off,

　the electromagnet loses its ....

Exercise 2 Writing two or more sentences in an answer

Sometimes, a question needs a slightly longer answer than usual. In this exercise, you practise writing your own sentences to answer some 'Explain' questions.

Look at **Command words** in the *English skills and support* section for information about command words.

Write at least **two** sentences to answer each of these three questions. Make sure that your second sentence has some new information in it and is not just the first sentence written in a different way.

a Explain how you can make an electromagnet.

....

....

....

....

b Explain how you can find out which is the north pole of an electromagnet.

....

....

....

....

c Explain **one** use of an electromagnet.

....

....

....

....

> 9.4 Investigating electromagnets

Exercise 1 Planning and doing an experiment

This exercise checks that you understand some of the vocabulary that we use when planning experiments.

Sofia and Zara want to find out if changing the number of cells in the circuit for their electromagnet changes the strength of the magnet.

a Suggest a hypothesis that the girls can test in their experiment.

....

....

b What is the variable that the girls change in their experiment?

....

c Describe how the girls can use paperclips to measure the dependent variable in their experiment.

....

....

....

d State **two** variables that the girls must keep the same in their experiment.

....

....

Exercise 2 Results and conclusions

This exercise is about the words we use to describe results charts and to complete them. It is also about using results to write a conclusion.

Look at **The language of science experiments** in the *English skills and support* section for information about results and conclusions.

Arun and Marcus did an experiment to test this hypothesis:

The more coils I use, the stronger the electromagnet I can make.

For each circuit, they counted how many paperclips their electromagnet could hold.

These are the results that they wrote down.

> 0 coils, 0 paperclips 5 coils, 2 paperclips 10 coils, 8 paperclips
> 15 coils, 12 paperclips 20 coils, 19 paperclips

a   In the space below, draw a table with two **columns** and six **rows**.

b   In your table, write the heading of the first column: number of coils

c   In your table, write a suitable heading for the second column.

d   Complete the results table by writing in the boys' results.

e   Write a conclusion that the boys can make, from the results of their experiment.

    ....

    ....